How to Pray Out Loud

by Coty Schwabe

How to Pray Out Loud
COPYRIGHT © 2023 by Coty Schwabe

Disclaimer: This is a work of nonfiction. The stuff shared is based on my own experience and has helped me but should not be taken as guidance or advice. I'm neither a pastor nor doctor or any other kind of suffixed "or". The information provided is purely for educational purposes. I'm just a guy that loves Jesus and wants to help people grow in their walk with Christ. That is it.

FIRST EDITION.
ISBN: 9798388574534 (Paperback)

thanks to God,
my wife Amanda,
Vineyard Church for my salvation,
and viewers like you

FREE AUDIOBOOK AT:

https://asoulredeemed.com/HowToPrayAudiobook

Table of Contents

Why We Should Be
Praying Out Loud

If you've been a Christian for any length of time, then you know that praying is an integral part of being a follower of Christ. There are so many verses about praying continuously (Luke 18:1), praying for others (1 Timothy 2:1), and all situations (Ephesians 6:18).

But I don't think it's something we do enough of.

Many of us consider prayer as a sort of "last resort." I've even heard pastors make the joke that when a situation arises, and they haven't prayed, they exclaim, "so it's come to this!"

A little more ironic is the number of Christians I have talked to that are literally afraid to *pray out loud*. They say things like "I pray in secret," or, "I pray when I'm alone."

And, while yes, this is something we should be doing (Matthew 6:6), it does not invalidate the fact we are also called to pray for others *in real time* and pray over things **out loud**.

There is power in praying for things out loud, as it gives us better access to the Holy Spirit and the work He wishes to do.

Moreover, we pray for things out loud, in person, in case there IS a change, so that we might see it occur and be encouraged, but also for others to see as well and learn from our example.

Another response I tend to get is, "well I'm constantly talking to God. I talk to Him to multiple times a day." Again. This is great. Staying in touch with your Father IS important.

But many times, praying out loud – especially in front of others – isn't about us. It's about being a light to others. It's about showing a real example of God in action.

What I've found to be the root reason of why people don't pray out loud is simply one thing: **Fear**.

Whether it's the fear of rejection or saying the wrong things or stalling during the prayer or seeing no result, ultimately it all leads to a weak outward prayer life.

And this is not how God intended us to be.

The Bible says we were not given a spirit of timidity, but one of *power, love, and discipline* (2 Timothy 1:7). God gave us the Holy Spirit that we might go out into the world and use the Holy Spirit via prayer to change lives for the better and bring the Kingdom of Heaven down to our sinful and fallen world.

My goal with this little book is to help equip you to start praying out loud *today*.

In the next few chapters, I'll share the template that I typically use – a format I've created over many years – so that you can at least have a starting point into praying out loud. It's a simple but honest and powerful template, that you can tweak, then abandon, once you get to the point where you no longer need it.

Of course, my way of praying is by no means the ONLY way to pray. However, I believe it will give you a good starting point. One that works for me and has worked well for others, too.

The last chapter will have some suggestions and tips for effective prayer, and things that I think will help bolster your confidence and make the whole thing a lot less stressful.

One final note that I'd like to leave you with is this:

Praying is just like anything else; you have to do it, to FEEL comfortable doing it. Over time, you'll be able to focus on what God wants to say or do through you while praying, as opposed to being focused on messing up.

In other words: You must do it to get better at it.

And we can't use the excuse of "not knowing how to pray," to not do so. I don't think that's going to go over well with the Big Guy when we meet Him face to face.

Jesus prayed out loud all the time, for all kinds of things: Lazarus, the storm, the fish and loaves, etc. And since Jesus is the

2

role model of what Christianity should be, we need to follow that example. And then we must *become* the example.

ONE FINAL REASON TO PRAY ALOUD

Praying for people and situations out loud is a simple, powerful way to talk to people about God or share the gospel.

For instance, many of us have given money to someone standing on a street corner, but how many of us have taken the time to actually pray with that person, too?

Sure, we should be sharing our money and resources with the less fortunate, we are called to do that (Proverbs 19:17, James 2:14-17). Our Father sees this and smiles.

However, how much better is it that we also pray for that individual <u>on top of the good deed</u>, that we may give God the glory and talk to that person about Him? Doing good deeds in Jesus' name is a great way for that person to come to Jesus.

What I've found is this:

Most people – whether they are religious or not – will accept prayer, especially when in a bad situation.

And I mean, why not? The risk/reward of receiving prayer is astronomical.

If nothing happens, they're not any worse off.

If God does move in that moment, it could be a life (or eternity) changer.

<u>The reward vastly outweighs the risk.</u>

In investing, we call this, "asymmetrical upside."

Good Deeds x Prayer = God's Work Accomplished

Money or service for someone is great, but it only makes this life a little less *miserable*. But prayer can change lives or souls.

You never know when the prayer is more impactful than the deed.

In fact, let me tell you a quick story that illustrates this point and happened very recently (and could be the basis for this very book!):

A few weeks ago, I drove up to our local grocery store to pick up a few things for the house.

When I pulled into the parking lot, I saw an older gentleman holding a cardboard sign that said, "anything helps."

I had some cash on me, so I parked, and made my way over to him.

I gave him the cash, which he graciously accepted, but while I was there, I asked if I could pray for him, which he replied, "of course."

I asked his name, and he gave it to me: Brian. Then he asked for my name, and I gave him it in return.

We call that a, "fair exchange."

So, he gave me a few things to pray about, and I stood there and prayed for him. He was very excited about it.

Well, nothing of major note happened, so after the prayer sesh, I bid him *adieu*, and went about my business.

About a week or so later, I happened to see him in the same spot when I arrived at the store again.

Now, I'll be honest here – this time, I didn't feel led to pray for him or give him more money. And I don't know if that was the Spirit not prompting me, or just my flesh getting in the way, but I just didn't feel anything.

But I did feel a little guilty not helping him in the store, so I made sure to pull out cash on the way out just in case something changed.

Quick side note: If you can, I've found that carrying some cash on you, even if it's a few bucks, is a good idea, since you can use that as the springboard to give to someone and then pray for them.

It's the bait for our prayer trap (lol).

Anyways, I left the store, and sure enough, this time I felt led to talk to him again. (Thanks a lot, God)

I put my groceries away, and went over to him, thinking nothing of it. We were just two strangers that happened to be in the same place, again. Probably coincidence.

I think not!

His face lit up when he saw me, and before I had even made it over to him, he said, "oh hey, Coty."

That kind of blew me away. I was so surprised.

See, I make it a big deal to remember people's names. At church, in small groups, in public, whatever – remembering people's names is such a great way to not only make them like you, but also to make them feel valued as a person. Our names are part of our identity. (This is a great tip I picked up from Dale Carnegie's *How to Win Friends and Influence People*)

In this instance, I had remembered the guy's name, but I was super surprised when he remembered mine! It made my day.

But here's the kicker...

He remembered *my name* – **because I had prayed for him!**

He said: "I just want to thank you. I really appreciate that you gave me money, but the prayer you prayed for me is really what helped me. It encouraged me."

I felt so humbled by that, you know?

So, I gave him the cash I had on hand, and I prayed for him again, and I haven't seen him since.

My point out of all of this is that praying for people is such an underrated yet powerful tool to show people the goodness of God.

Even if we don't see anything change right in that moment (like we do on TV), that doesn't mean it can't bring encouragement or hope to someone who is going through something tough.

And who knows if God won't move in their situations later when we aren't there to see the plants grow from the seeds we have sown. We don't know who will turn to God because of our small sacrifice of time for them.

5

Like I said earlier, we should be praying for people and things constantly.

And especially praying out loud.

We have to get past those feelings of outward prayer being awkward or weird or whatever.

It doesn't matter.

We need to step out of that comfort zone.

I personally like to push people out of their comfort zone by having them pray aloud for simple things like gatherings or meals to get them used to doing so.

Prayer is important and should be ingrained in us. It should be the first thing we turn to in a situation, not a last resort.

Are you ready?

Just Follow GRACE

The easiest way to begin praying out loud is by following a template. The template I'll be showing you isn't meant to be the "end-all be-all" of praying, nor is it the only "correct" way to pray.

But the structure I'll be providing is simple to follow and easy to replicate.

It's also not hard to remember as I have written its key components in the following acrostic: GRACE

GIVE thanks
RECEIVE the Spirit
(Be) AUTHENTIC
(Be) CONCISE
END Naturally

I know, I know…

It's a little on the nose. A little cheesy.

But here's the thing: That's what came to me, and I'm sticking with it.

Each component exemplifies a step in the prayer, and are, for the most part, in order.

However, as you pray more and more, and allow the Spirit to move, the way that you pray over time will probably change. That's okay.

My goal is just to get you started.

AN ARGUMENT AGAINST STRUCTURED PRAYERS

Before I start breaking down the structure I use, let me address a common argument against using structured, pre-written, or reused prayer elements.

There are many people (and pastors) who argue that saying the same things over and over again in your prayers basically cheapens them; it makes them less effective.

And to this I agree… **IF you're only going through the motions.**

But if you're just starting out, and you aren't that confident in praying, having a model to follow will help you feel more confident, and give you something to go off of.

My other argument for this is:

Everything that deals with God, *is a matter of the heart.* He knows the intention of everything we do.

So if you're just saying the prayer just to say it, that's a heart issue, not a mouth issue.

The words aren't the problem—<u>you are.</u>

You can reuse elements of a prayer repeatedly – I do. They can still be used by God.

I'm pretty sure God would have us pray for people, even if we've prayed the same prayer before especially if it makes a difference in that person's life.

Is that an excuse to be lazy? Of course not. You should pray as you feel led, using the most effective words you can think of.

As you pray over time, you'll find your own rhythms and styles and words to use, and you'll probably find yourself reusing phrases without thinking about it – just like in normal conversation.

Don't overthink it.

Any prayer is good as long as it is genuine.

GIVE Thanks

The very first thing I do when I go to pray for someone, is to give thanks to God (the Father). Literally, I will open my prayers with, "Father, I thank you." That is my first line of dialogue.

I thank God for 2 things:

1)   For the opportunity to pray
2)   For what He is already doing (or has done)

Let's address the first thing.

I love praying out loud. Whether it's for people or meals or gatherings or events, praying is my favorite. (Like singing is to Buddy in *Elf*)

Depending on what it is that I'm praying about, I will simply thank God for the opportunity to pray for that person or thing:

"Thank you, Lord, for allowing me to pray for Linda…"
"Thank you, Father, for this meal…"

Then, I immediately follow that up with the second part of thanking God for what He is already doing in the situation or people's lives.

"…and I thank you for what you are already doing for her/him/us/this situation."

The reason I start with this is because not only does the Bible tell us to give thanks to God in all circumstances (1 Thessalonians 5:18), but also **because it's a solemn reminder of God's goodness, even in tough situations.**

I start my prayers with thanks because if it weren't for God, we (you and I) wouldn't even be here connecting, via this book.

Doing this helps anchor us in the present, and to remind us that God is always working things out for our good (Romans 8:28). Sometimes we just need to be reminded of that.

Think about all the miracles God performed for the Israelites i.e., helping them escape Egypt, parting the Red Sea, and raining manna down from the sky…

They still complained and grumbled and forgot all of those amazing things in such a short amount of time!

How easily we forget the good things that have happened in our lives over time.

By opening our prayers with thanks, we are not just centering the prayer on our request alone but acknowledging what God has done in the past.

RECEIVE the Holy Spirit

Next is to receive the Holy Spirit. Really, it's invite, but that doesn't start with 'R', *so receive it is*!

Here, I will invite the Holy Spirit to come and dwell with us so that God's work can be done.

I'll say something like, "come Holy Spirit, and be with us."

That simple.

The reason we do this next is because the Holy Spirit is both God's messenger and laborer. It is how God instructs and empowers His people to do His Will.

While God does seem to get involved in external (physical) circumstances, most of the time, the internal (personal) work is done via the Spirit.

By inviting the Spirit, we are giving Him a chance to work. We are also told that the Spirit is with us when 2 or more are gathered in His name. (Matthew 18:20)

If we just jump right into the meat of the prayer, without asking for the Holy Spirit's help, we can often miss opportunities that God has laid out for us. We become so focused on the task of just praying and being done with it, that we miss what the Spirit wants to do, which could be completely different.

BEING PROMPTED

If you don't think you've ever been prompted by the Holy Spirit, you probably have but didn't know it.

Generally, if you've ever had the feeling that you should be doing something for someone else – like praying or giving money or serving somehow – then it was probably the Holy Spirit.

If you see someone struggling, and you get the sudden urge to help them – especially if you haven't helped them before – that's probably the Spirit prompting you.

It's also why, depending on whether you responded or not, you feel a certain way.

For example: Maybe you did help someone, and you felt that joy — that sense of accomplishment or pride or love — afterwards. Like you did good.

That's the Holy Spirit reaffirming you.

Or maybe you didn't help. You let fear or busyness or some other excuse stop you, and afterwards you felt convicted, and it weighed on your heart for a while.

Just know that this feeling isn't necessarily a feeling of condemnation, but rather a point for us to reflect and try to hear (and obey) the Spirit more clearly.

By inviting the Holy Spirit, we are both allowing Him to prompt us with God's messages, AND give Him a chance to move in whatever situation we're praying about.

And, in turn, the prompting empowers us too.

With the power of the Holy Spirit active in us, we are able to do the works that Jesus did. That's the whole point of the Spirit.

That thought always amazes me: **we have access to the same Holy Spirit that Jesus did.**

Crazy.

Be AUTHENTIC

This component is less of an action per se, and more of a guiding principle. It pertains to the "meat" of the prayer.

Essentially, every prayer is one thing: **A request from us to God to do something.**

What you actually say in this part of the prayer will obviously change depending on what it is you're praying about.

However, the thing that a lot of people get hung up on when it comes to this part of the prayer, is "using the right words."

They don't know what to say.

And that's okay. I've got the remedy.

You ready to hear it?

Ok. Here it is:

Just talk like you naturally would to anyone else.

Look, while God is the creator of Heaven and Earth, He is also our Father. And the way you would talk to your regular dad (or mom) is exactly how you should talk to your Heavenly Father.

Just have a conversation with Him. That's it.

Your prayers don't have to be overly flowy or sound super smart and educated or use the best words—it just has to be from the heart.

It doesn't have to be perfect...

It just has to be genuine.

Here's the thing: Many of us look at pastors or preachers on TV and they seem to have these charismatic or powerful sounding prayers. And we think, "wow, they sound so good. I just sound like a mumbling idiot."

But that's okay. Everyone prays differently because everyone speaks differently.

God is more concerned with your intent than your façade.

If you haven't caught on, God is more interested with our heart (motives) than He is with how we appear to others.

He told Samuel this in 1 Samuel 16:7 when he said:

"Do not consider his appearance or his height, for I have rejected him. The Lord does not look at the things people look at. People look at the outward appearance, but the Lord looks at the heart." (NIV)

This is a repeating theme with God throughout the Bible. It's why Jesus called the scribes and Pharisees "whitewashed tombs" (Matthew 23:27), said not to practice our righteousness or prayer for attention (Matthew 6:1, 6:5), and told the crowds not to babble like Gentiles to sound sophisticated (Matthew 6:7).

So when it comes to praying, it's just about being yourself.

And even I – someone who isn't afraid to pray in public – still mess up my words or forget what I'm saying or repeat things. I'm not perfect. But so what? There's no such thing as perfection (aside from Christ).

God already knows what our request is before we even make it. (Matthew 6:8)

All you need to do at this point is to just go ahead and ask your Father to do the thing you're asking be done.

For instance, if I were praying for healing, I'd say at this point:

"Father I just ask that you heal So&So's leg in the name of Jesus. I pray that you take the pain away and mend whatever is going on within it."

You don't need to sit there and try to sound perfect. You don't need to "say the right words." Just say whatever sounds right.

This leads me to the next part of the acrostic, **being concise.**

Be CONCISE

When praying, you don't need to use extra words to "fluff out" your prayer because you feel like you haven't said enough. This isn't a high school essay where you need to add words to meet a quota.

You also don't need to use a bunch of synonyms to describe the same thing for emphasis.

There's a joke that Christian comedian Tim Hawkins makes about what he calls "thesaurus prayers:" people who use multiple words for the same point, as if to emphasize it.

They say things like "Lord, lead us... guide us... direct us... navigate for us... show us the way..."

And I've heard these prayers myself.

Now, I don't say this to be mean, and I think many Christians are simply insecure about their prayers, so they stumble and use filler words to make their prayers sound a little more important or little less discombobulated.

You don't need to do this.

You just need to get to the point.

I mentioned this a few pages ago:

Jesus spoke out against "babbling like pagans, for they think they will be heard because of their many words." (Matthew 6:7 NIV)

The religious leaders of Jesus' day also did this: They would pray these loud, eloquent prayers so that people would be impressed with their "amazing speech." But the prayers weren't impressing the one person that mattered: God.

He's not fooled by our many words or eloquent speeches.

He just wants us to acknowledge Him, make our request, and leave it in His hands.

That's it.

Now, yes, you can elaborate on the topic of the prayer. Having specific things to pray for is better than something generic. Praying for healing of a broken bone is better than just praying for "good health."

Or if there are additional aspects to what you were praying for, then you can pray for those additional things.

For instance: if I was praying for someone overcoming addiction, I might pray for strength against temptation, for God to put people and resources in their path to help them, and against Satan's attacks over them (more on this later).

PRAYING OVER AND OVER AGAIN

I'd like to throw in one exception to the rule above, and that is praying for healing.

Many times, when you pray for physical healing on someone, you won't see a change right away. This doesn't mean that God isn't listening, nor does it mean they won't be healed later on. (And sadly, they may not be healed at all, but more on that later.)

WE don't make that determination. God does.

However, there will be those awesome instances where you pray for healing, and you actually DO see a positive result in real time. Maybe the person starts to see after being blind for a long time or a pain in their body starts to dissipate.

In this case, you actually WOULD continue to pray for that person, inviting more of God's healing on them.

If the Holy Spirit is moving in that moment, why would we want to stop that?

Basically a "fly with the wind," situation.

Here, I would just thank God for moving, invite more of His presence, and ask Him to continue to heal that person.

"Holy Spirit, I thank you, for healing Jane's arm. We ask for more of your presence, and that you continue to heal this broken arm; that you would mend the bones and take away the inflammation."

As long as the person continues to improve, continue to pray. Once they reach a point where nothing changes after a few minutes, then go ahead and end the prayer.

Even Jesus had instances where He healed people in stages, such as the man who was blind and He used his saliva to give him sight. The first time, the man could only see "trees." The second time his vision was fully restored. (Mark 8:22-25)

Again, you may not see full restoration for that person (as much as you might want to). It's okay. It's not our job to heal the person, just to obey God. Don't get discouraged.

END Naturally

Once you've made your points to God, it's simply time to end the prayer.

So many people just stumble around at the end of prayer, not knowing how to close it out.

It's simple: Just end it.

Literally, once you have made your requests to God, and you don't feel the Holy Spirit prompting you to pray about anything else, simply say the following:

"And we pray these things in Jesus name, amen."

That's all you have to do.

There are times when I feel the Holy Spirit very strongly, and I will pray very fervently, and then, all of a sudden I won't feel the Holy Spirit anymore. And instead of trying to keep the prayer going, I just close up shop right then and there.

Honestly, you can close a prayer however you'd like.

The reason I end my prayers in Jesus' name is because He is my example and I am His disciple, so I'm asking for His help in accomplishing whatever it is I'm praying about.

However, you can end in the Father's name, or even use nothing if you'd like. Whatever is most comfortable for you.

Most of the prayers in the Bible just end in "amen," even the Lord's Prayer, so it's perfectly fine to do.

And you're done.

See? That wasn't so hard was it?

Conclusion

Praying, like anything else worth doing, takes practice to become comfortable and confident in doing it.

You must get out there and actually do it to get over that mental block.

I think a lot of people have this idea that praying out loud, especially in a group of people, is like a "mini public speaking gig."

While it is kind of similar to a speaking gig in the fact that it's in public, the difference is: <u>praying is not about us</u>.

Praying is about the people and situations we're praying for. That should be our motivation to do it.

It's easy to get in your own head and overthink it, but as I've said before: It's just a conversation to your dad, asking Him to help you with something.

Asking God for help should be as easy as saying, "Hey, dad. Just wondering if you could help Jim here with his marriage. It's kinda falling apart here, and we were just wondering if you could help him fix it. Thanks."

People who can pray well are ones who are well practiced in praying. That's just how it works.

But I think with the framework I've given you; you can at least get started. Just remember GRACE.

In the next chapter, I've included an example of a prayer I created just for this book, with some notes included.

Afterwards, the next chapter has some suggestions and notes that I wanted to include but didn't feel they EXACTLY fit in a specific part of GRACE, so I have appended them there.

Thank you for reading this short little book, and I'm excited for your progress. If you'd like to let me know how it's going, you can message me on Twitter or Instagram or visit my site, https://cotyschwabe.com. I'd love to hear your thoughts and progress.

God bless and good prayers.

Example Prayer

Now I'd like to give you an example of a prayer that I would pray for the healing of a sprained ankle. I'm going to make it up on the spot, so that you can see how natural, genuine, and concise praying can be.

Here it is:

###

"Father, I thank you so much for the opportunity to pray for Linda's sprained ankle, and I thank you for everything you're already doing for her in her life.

"Holy Spirit, I just pray that you would come, hear us, and move.

"Right now, in the name of Jesus, I pray for healing on this ankle. I pray that you would take this pain and cast it out.

"Holy Spirit I pray that you would bring absolute healing on this entire foot. That you repair the ligaments and tendons that were damaged in this accident, and I pray for a faster than normal recovery.

"And I pray that you would bring that healing right now, Jesus.

"Father, I also pray for anything else going on in Linda's life right now that she hasn't thought to share with me, but that you know about. *

"I pray for the pain and the struggles she is currently facing. And even though she might not have brought it to you, I'm bringing it to you on her behalf. **

"So Father, I just pray for more of your healing, and these situations, and ultimately more of your love upon Linda. I pray that you continue to be here for her and remind her that she is not alone in the challenges she's facing, and that you are on her side.

"I thank you again for letting me pray for her, and I say these things in Jesus' name, amen."

\### \### \###

*(This line is twofold: 1) In case there is anything else they want prayer for, while we're at it, & 2) that the Holy Spirit would prompt if the person doesn't say anything, but God puts it on my heart.)

**(Sometimes, we just forget to pray about things, especially things we consider trivial. I try to be that ambassador and bring things to God for them as their example to also do so on their own.)

You'll notice that there are points where I repeat words, like addressing God multiple times. This is simply a personal habit. I tend to do this, but you can omit multiple instances of God/Jesus/Holy Spirit.

Notes and Suggestions

In this section, I'd like to offer some suggestions and notes that while not necessary to follow, I think they will help you become more confident a lot faster and pray more effectively.

PRACTICE MAKES PERFECT

Just like anything else in life, practice makes perfect here. To get good, you have to do it.

If you're worried about people judging you about your prayers, the easiest way to start is by yourself. Get comfortable praying out loud alone, about whatever subjects you can think about or on your heart, and simply practice as if someone else was there with you.

Once you've done it a few times, then pray for people close to you that you know won't judge you if nothing happens or would act awkward about you praying for them.

Afterwards, you can start praying for acquaintances (people you know, but aren't real close to) if possible. Neighbors, coworkers, people at church or nearby. Whatever.

Then onto strangers. Of course, you must use caution and care when asking certain people to pray for them – such as homeless people – as I have no judgment against them, but you also don't know their history.

What I recommend in the case of praying for strangers is to do it when someone you know is with you, or in the very least, praying for strangers in an open, public place with a lot of vision.

Lastly, you can then pray in groups. Groups of four to five or less is a good place to start, then you can move up from there. Easy ways to practice here is for Thanksgiving dinners, church events, serving opportunities, workdays, etc.

Look, if you can pray for one person, you can pray for a thousand. It's all the same.

Earlier I mentioned how some people equate praying out loud to public speaking. They do share similarities, with the biggest being that <u>most people are deathly afraid of messing up in front of other people.</u>

I, too, was afraid of this when I was younger.

I'd get super nervous in front of people.

Then one day, many years ago, I was asked to do a talk for our youth group of a couple hundred kids.

My nerves were wracked, and my stomach was upset, and I was sweaty all over. I didn't want to do it, even in the last few minutes leading up to the event.

But I realized something important – it wasn't about me.

The talk and the prayer was for the audience. For the youth. And I needed to do it, whether I liked it or not. Whether I was ready or not.

I had to face that fear to get over it.

And so I did. I gave my "sermon."

And to be honest…

It wasn't great. It was okay. Mediocre, at best.

But I did it.

The first few minutes were the worst. But once I was actually doing it, it got easier.

The next time I gave a talk in youth, it was a little easier. Less nerves, and hesitation. Still some, sure.

But I had "survived" the first time, I could do it again.

And the second talk was better. Easier.

After that, I was asked to give a groomsman speech. Had no idea how to give one. I scraped together a bunch of templates I found online, wrote out a script, and delivered it the day of the wedding. I thought I did pretty well.

A few years later, I was asked to officiate my friend's wedding. I had never done anything like that! But I was excited, and it was one of those things that you feel bad if you say no to.

So I agreed. I wrote my own script and everything using more templates I found on Google (thank God for the internet), and some tips from a close pastor friend.

The day came and…

I officiated the heck out of that wedding! It went exactly as we had hoped. No flaws (and boy am I grateful for that).

But I was still nervous to do it. A lot of strangers judging me for their family member's special day.

But I didn't let the fear stop me. I had to do it to get over it.

Lastly, another friend of ours committed suicide a few years ago. It was a great tragedy, and I still miss him dearly.

I was asked to speak at the funeral. Again, another instance of speaking in front of 100+ people. And I did. I wrote another script and delivered it.

People afterwards even came up to me and said they appreciated what I had said in my speech. They remarked it had been well said. Not that I'm proud about the event, but it just shows that practice improves form.

I just followed a script I wrote out, practiced it a few times (both alone and in front of my wife), and then I delivered it. It's simple.

My point out of all of this is that you can't let fear stop you from doing what's right. We are called to pray for all kinds of things and all kinds of people. Whether we're comfortable with it or not.

If you're still nervous, just follow the template and structure I've provided and use it over and over again, until you feel it needs to be changed.

Like my first talk in our church's youth program all those years ago – saying something and looking kind of lame is still better than not speaking up at all when it needs to be done.

Just get out there and get your hands dirty.

THINK KISS

Like I've said before, don't overthink it. Just remember KISS.

No, not the rock band. The acronym:

Keep It Simple Silly. (There is another word I could use for silly but I won't use it here)

Although I have provided a template here and structure suggestions, ultimately, it's all just a springboard for you to get some momentum from.

The style you use to pray will be based largely on how you genuinely communicate AND how you've seen others model prayer.

Your first prayers will sound lame or have a ton of repetition or long pauses.

That's okay.

As long as you keep the prayer *genuine, concise, and Spirit-led,* you'll do fine.

The Bible says that the Spirit interprets what we're trying to say to God. He knows us. And so does God.

Keep it simple.

COMMANDING AGAINST SATAN AND FOR JESUS

So here's the thing:

God is in charge of everything. We both know this.

What you may not know is that since we have access to the Holy Spirit, we also have the power of God via the Holy Spirit.

It's kinda like our superpower as Christians.

(Sorry, Spider-Man.)

It's our link to God. Our indwelt embodiment of Christ.

And because we have this power, we can command the power of the Spirit in two ways:

1.	Commanding Satan and demons to leave
2.	Commanding action in the name of Jesus

Let's take the first one.

Since the power of the Holy Spirit is our supernatural power from God, we have an advantage over Satan and his minions.

Satan, while conniving, has no power like the Holy Spirit. It's easy to think of Satan as this all-powerful, demigod-like creature with the ability to control fire and suck people down into Hell. We think of him as a Disney villain.

The truth couldn't be further.

Satan has very little actual power. The one power he does have, however, is the power of persuasion. And he is good at it.

So good he uses our own inadequacies against us. Manipulates us with bad ideas and thoughts and temptations.

But that's the extent of his power.

The power of the Holy Spirit is lightyears more powerful than Satan's mind tricks.

We just rarely access it, so we don't really know that.

It's like Luke Skywalker being able to wield the Force, but not knowing he could 'cause he wasn't trained to do it. He had to practice and trust that he could do it in order to harness its power.

Now, because the Holy Spirit has *actual power*, we can wield it as both a sword and a shield. We can use it to shield ourselves from the enemy's attacks, but even more importantly, in the context of prayer, we can use it as a weapon against Satan.

Since Satan and his minions (demons) aren't physical beings, but rather spiritual ones, we have to fight them with a spiritual power. Fight fire with fire. (Although water is more effective in the metaphor. I digress.)

Empowered by the Spirit, we have the power and the authority (in Jesus' name) to tell Satan (and his demons) to leave us when we are being tempted or spiritually attacked.

How do we know if we are under spiritual attack?

Generally, the attacks are things that stop you from growing closer to God. Events that stop you from going to church or reading your Bible or making it to Bible study or praying for people or giving money to various causes (or tithing).

Because we have that *Holy Spirit Power* (lol), we can command Satan to leave us alone.

We simply say:

"Leave me, Satan. In the name of Jesus. You have no power here."

I like to add that last part as both a slight to Satan's lack of actual power but also as a reminder to myself that persuasion and attacks are all he has. He can't MAKE me do anything.

Speaking of spiritual attacks, remember when Jesus said something similar to the above statement?

It was when Peter was saying that Jesus shouldn't go to Jerusalem to be crucified. What was Jesus' reply?

"Get behind me, Satan! You are a stumbling block to me; you do not have in mind the concerns of God, but merely human concerns." (Matthew 16:23)

Peter probably wasn't expecting that response.

But Jesus tells Satan to get behind him (or to get out of his way, essentially).

Satan can try and get in our way, but he ain't in control.

Just remember that.

This is also true for demons. Demons are beneath God, Jesus, and the Spirit, and thus when it comes to them, the same rules apply.

Even the demons must obey God. It is why we, as normal people, can cast them out…

…but only with the power of the Spirit.

This is why Jesus was able to cast out many demons while He was on Earth. He was filled with the Holy Spirit. And as I mentioned before, we now have the same Holy Spirit dwelling within us.

It is omniscient and ubiquitous.

This brings me to the second part of commanding via the Spirit; *commanding things in Jesus' name.*

Although we are using the Holy Spirit as the means to accomplish the works of God, sometimes I find it helpful **commanding things in the name of Jesus**. Things like healing, breaking bondages of sin, or casting out demons.

The reason for this is because Jesus was our example. And He was the first one to be able to do such things on command using the Spirit. Other figures in the Bible have had the Spirit rest upon them, but it never dwelt IN them like it did in the Son of God.

Commanding things in Jesus' name isn't totally necessary, and many don't do it.

The reason I'm suggesting it here is because it adds power to the prayer. It gives the request *authority.*

I've mentioned before, that when we pray, the whole point is just that we are being obedient in bringing requests to God. Whether God answers those requests or not, is up to Him.

But when it comes to praying, we should take it seriously. We shouldn't just give a half-hearted prayer that languishes and has little drive behind it. If you were making a request to your parents or your boss or someone you loved, and you really, really wanted something from them, you wouldn't just throw the request out there and let it flounder.

You'd ask with heart. With gusto. With passion.

I recommend you do the same with prayer.

I've heard a lot of prayers out there that are just... flat. Monotone. Routine. Like the person is just making the prayer because they're forced to or put on the spot.

And look – I'm not judging them or bashing them. Especially people who are new to it.

But if you've been a Christian any length of time, you should be praying for circumstances and people. It's literally what we're called to do.

And if you truly love God, wouldn't that reflect in your prayers to Him?

Remember we don't *HAVE to pray.*

<u>We GET to pray.</u>

We get to talk to our dad, and we get to talk to Him with other people.

How cool is that?

I dunno, I'm getting carried away. I just love praying. I love God.

What can I say?

Use the superpower you've got to your advantage. Command Satan to leave and pray with authority in Jesus' name.

Easy peasy.

EYES OPEN OR EYES CLOSED?

One of the questions a lot of new Christians will ask is:

Should I pray with my eyes open or closed?

If you're by yourself, it doesn't really matter.

But if you're praying for someone, I have a practical answer.

Generally, the consensus I've heard, and we practice this in our church, is that the person praying will keep their eyes open, while the person being prayed for, will close theirs.

The main reason is so you don't have any weird moments where you're staring into each other's eyes while you're praying.

It's distracting in the very least.

I typically have the person receiving prayer close their eyes or at least bow their head for this reason. This also allows them to receive without distraction.

The reason we – as the prayer(er)s – keep our eyes open is so that we can see if the Spirit is moving.

Since the Spirit is the one doing the heavy lifting here, and we don't know how God will move when we pray for someone, we want to be open to it, and look for signs of activity.

Hints that God is moving in that person.

For example, if we pray for healing on say their arm, and we're holding it, and we see the muscles move involuntarily, then it's possible God is healing them *in real time*. We would confirm this by asking if they felt anything.

Another thing we look for is tears, heat, or shivers. This can mean that the Spirit of God is resting on them, and in this junction, we want to ask for more of the Holy Spirit to continue His work. We don't want to shut off the Spirit's work prematurely.

The last thing we look for is demonic activity. This one takes a little more discernment to uncover, and you may need help if that's the case. What tends to happen is the person usually will shake or convulse when you start praying for them (but not always). They may also get super angry or start screaming. If this happens, it's best to have someone pray with you or at least be present for your (and the receiving person's) safety. In fact, I'd recommend it.

But if you're rolling solo – and they are possessed but you feel safe enough to proceed – then you just got to ask the Lord for protection and cast that thing out into the abyss. You don't need to know its name, just keep saying something along the lines of "I bind you unclean spirit in the name of Jesus Christ, and command you to leave and go to the abyss."

It might be scary but listen to me – God's Spirit is greater. God is in control. Nothing happens that He does not allow.

So pray with your eyes open when praying for others.

(Side note: Isaiah Saldivar is great pastor with some in-depth deliverance videos on YouTube. I'll mention him again shortly.)

BE LED BY THE SPIRIT

Piggybacking off the last point, when we pray, we should be open to what the Spirit wants to do. Maybe what things to say or topics to mention.

If you're unsure about what to pray about - it might be awkward at first - but you can ask our buddy, the Holy Spirit, what to pray about.

Even if you have specific topics to pray about for a person or situation, that doesn't mean there isn't something else that God wants you to bring before Him.

Usually, it's something the recipient forgets to ask for prayer for. Or it could be a hidden sin (or past event) they're ashamed of.

Whatever the case, if we consistently ask the Spirit to come and dwell with us, generally we can be led in the direction He wants to go.

The promptings could come as a voice from nowhere or an image or words in your mind. God speaks in many different ways.

For me, it's usually like an actual typewritten text that appears in my mind. Almost as if I were reading a note from Him.

Here's an example:

I was praying for my wife's friend. She had just had a baby, but the baby was sick and had to stay in the hospital. They said it might be up to a month.

When I was praying for her, I saw the words "ten days."

I said, "I see the words ten days. I think it means that your baby will come home within ten days of today."

Nine days later, the baby came home.

She called my wife freaking out. But it was a great witness story for God.

Praying for things and people is good. We should be doing it, "without ceasing" (1 Thessalonians 5:17) daily.

But we shouldn't just get into the routine of having a topic, getting our prayer in, and ducking out before the Spirit has a chance to move. This isn't a James Bond rescue mission.

I like to give the Spirit at least a minute or so – when I can – to give me any further promptings before I end the prayer.

Sometimes the Spirit doesn't really prompt us to do or say anything else. Maybe we pray about something, then we give the Spirit a moment for further promptings, and nothing happens.

That's okay.

We just need to be open to it.

MAKE IT PERSONAL

One thing we want to avoid as Christians is saying the same prayers over and over again without deviation or personality or uniqueness. If you simply say the same prayer repeatedly, it's easy for the prayer to become a routine that loses its meaning. You'll just be "going through the motions of prayer."

The danger in bringing stale, dead prayer to a situation is like giving the same response to various people who ask the same question. You can do it, but it holds very little value.

Just saying "good," to everyone when they ask how you're doing doesn't invite a real response.

To combat this, we need to make our prayers personal.

What do I mean by personal?

Make prayer personal by adding in things you would normally do in conversation with a friend.

For instance, since God is our Father, sometimes I'll say "dad" in my prayer. Or I'll start my sentences like I would a casual conversation: "Listen, Lord…" or "Jesus, all I'm asking…"

I can't harp enough to be natural in your prayers. Just say what needs to be said and stop worrying about saying the perfect words.

The other part to this is making it personal to the person themselves.

If you know the person, and some of the struggles they are dealing with, include them in the prayer. (However, if those struggles are deeply personal, then only do it if Spirit led. Otherwise, you can pray for God's intervention into anything else they are dealing with without being specific.)

If you don't know the person, one thing I'll typically say in the prayer is that God loves them and has already done so much for them. This is kind of a way for me to be able to implant the idea to them that God has been with them all along. You don't have to, but this is just a personal thing I do that helps them see God has never abandoned them, even through difficult situations.

Personal prayer just means making it your own, and highlighting details about the person or situation that stick out to you, even if they don't seem like a big deal. God puts different things on different people's hearts.

EXPECT GOD TO MOVE

One thing that has helped me recently in strengthening my prayers – both for myself and for others – is to have the mindset going into the prayer *that God is going to move.*

In the past, I would just show up and start praying, hoping that God would do something. And I'm not saying He can't regardless of our attitude or heart posture. God is sovereign, He can do what He wants.

I'd say something like, "… and if you want to God, then you'll do this..."

However, there's something to be said about expecting God to move in some way because it requires us to *have faith* that He will.

I have two scriptures to back up this claim:

And whatever you ask in prayer, you will receive, if you have faith. (Matthew 21:22 ESV)

AND

Now faith is confidence in what we hope for and assurance about what we do not see. (Hebrews 11:1 ESV)

Essentially, if we boil down what prayer is (to recap earlier chapters) it's simply us talking to our dad about stuff. And more often than not, it's 'submitting a request' to Him.

And if we go into a prayer with little or no expectation of moving, then doesn't that show a lack of faith on our part?

The above verses emphasize one continuous point:

That we "will receive what we asked for in faith" and "confidently hope for."

Based on this, it stands to reason that we should expect God to not only hear our prayer, but do something.

Again – it's not a guarantee that He WILL move, especially how we are expecting Him to.

However, having this mindset not only gives you more confidence when 'approaching the throne of God,' but it gives your prayers more *authority*.

What I've found recently is that by having this attitude when I pray for people or situations, it has helped me strengthen my faith as a result.

It's cyclical, actually.

By having faith that God will move, the faith is fortified – whether we see Him move or not, I feel more obedient in the doing, regardless of the result. And when He does move, it only reemphasizes the approach!

One last note: I'm not suggesting we start yelling at people or demanding that God do things for us. This is different than commanding things in Jesus' name like casting out demons or healing people. We simply expect that God will move in response to our request and pray assuming He will. That's it.

SHARING A MINI-GOSPEL

One of my favorite reasons for praying with people is because it's an easy (and effective) way to share the gospel.

The great commission (found in Matthew 28:16-20) commands all followers of Jesus to "go and make disciples, baptizing them, and teaching them."

It's not just for pastors, evangelists, and missionaries...

It's for all of us.

Now, I understand that many believers don't know how to go about doing this. We're unsure of what means or methods we should be utilizing to share our testimony, beliefs, or faith with others.

It could also be that we have reservations about doing so. Maybe it's a fear of rejection or of public opinion or feelings of inadequacy.

Regardless, I get it. I really do. It's a tall order.

But I'd like to counter with two points:

1. If we have received the gift of salvation – by extension, eternal life – why would we not want to share that with others? There is no gift greater.
2. Are these things truly valid excuses to say before God on Judgment Day as to why we didn't follow His commands?

My goal here isn't to scare anyone. I, too, have struggled with sharing my faith with others. Even though I pray more than most people I know, I'm not immune to being stifled when it comes to witnessing.

Yet, there are only so many pastors. So many preachers and evangelists and missionaries. Each one can only reach so many people.

We, too, must be sharing the "Good News" (gospel) with the people around us.

And if they don't accept it? Then we can rest easy knowing we did our part.

My goal here today is the opposite: I want to give you a strategy to easily share your faith.

This is something God revealed to me while I was filming a YouTube video recently for my channel, *A Soul Redeemed*.

While I was filming the video, and I was talking about why prayer was so important, the Lord revealed to me this simple strategy that blended both *my love for prayer* with *our command to share the faith*.

Ready to hear it? I'm still excited about it.

And I plan on using it for everyone that I'm not sure is saved.

Here it is:

Incorporate a mini gospel into your prayer.

See, when most people accept prayer, they're giving you an opportunity to speak to them about God.

And while we should, of course, invite the Holy Spirit into the prayer session, as well as pray for the things that person asked for, we also have a small window of opportunity to share with them the Good News of Jesus Christ.

I'm not saying you have to beat them over the head with it or recite the entire Bible from creation to Revelation (for when words abound, sin is near – Proverbs 10:19). In fact, you can summarize with just a few sentences, like such:

"Father, I thank you that you love Jane so much that you sent your one and only son, Jesus, to die for her on a cross, take away her sins, and secure her a spot in eternity with you forever should she accept it."

And there it is.

Is this a perfect, flawless strategy? No. Many will hear this and it'll go in one ear and out the other.

But does it plant a seed? Is it better than nothing? Does it give them something to think about?

Yes, yes, and yes.

While this shouldn't replace us sharing our testimony or our faith, it's a great way to supplement it, especially when the person is defensive or you have little time with them.

I think one of the reasons I love prayer so much is that it's so *disarming* and *unassuming*.

If you attempt to preach the gospel or evangelize, many listeners will grow defensive or combative. The majority are simply indifferent – which is arguably worse.

Yet a lot of folks are open to prayer. Even nonbelievers. In fact, I'm surprised by how many people I've come across that allowed me to pray for them; even if it was about something simple. Prayer doesn't feel like an overt attack on their beliefs.

Another cool thing about this 'strategy' is that it's *targeted*. When you ask someone if you can pray for them (and they say, 'yes'), you already have their permission to mention God!

Contrast this to messages about Him that people are tuned out of, and you already have a massive advantage! We've got to take advantage of every edge we can in sharing the love of Christ to the nations!

That opportunity is a special chance to not only encourage that person with the help of the Spirit, but to share the message of Christ in a genuine way that they may never receive otherwise!

You could be that person that gets them to desire a relationship with God that they never would have wanted in the first place.

How cool is that?

I get excited talking about it.

Listen – you don't have to do this every time. And you don't have to do it with people you know are saved.

But if you know that you are called to share more (as all of us are), you have now been given one simple method of doing so.

DON'T BE DISCOURAGED

The final and probably greatest piece of advice I could give you in this little book is to not be discouraged.

It's easy to be downtrodden or bummed out if you pray for a situation or person that doesn't ultimately work out like you'd hoped.

This is especially true with praying for healing, and someone doesn't get healed. Maybe they get worse. Or die.

It's easy to feel defeated and the enemy wants us to feel this way. He wants us to think that prayer is pointless just because things don't go the way we had hoped.

But God does as He pleases. And as hard as that might be to accept, it's true. While we wish we could heal every person and fix every wrong, it doesn't work like that.

That's life.

But keep praying. Keep praying for good outcomes of things. God hears every prayer and the Bible does say He answers them in His own way.

Remember: Prayer isn't about what we want.

It's about what God wants.

We submit the request, because that's our role.

Beyond that, it's up to Him.

Just keep praying.

All the time, for everything.

Appendix A: Praying in Tongues

Initially, the book ended with that last section. But I wrote this book over a year ago, and at the time, I didn't speak (or pray, rather) in tongues.

Now I do.

Personally, I've found it to be IMMENSELY gratifying and helpful in my conversations with God in my personal time.

If you've made it this far, and you're not interested in speaking in tongues (or other gifts after this) – then go ahead and stop reading. The book is complete, and I wish you the best.

However, if you'd like some general guidance on speaking in tongues and want to hear about my experience in it, then venture onward.

SHOULD WE SPEAK IN TONGUES?

For the longest time, I didn't believe that I needed – or even wanted – the gift of tongues. I figured that if God wanted me to have it, then it would just come upon me.

I had this thought for a long time.

However, I have found that while, yes, this can happen for some, most of the people I have watched or know that can do it, had to put in "effort" to get it.

What do I mean by that?

Glad you asked.

See, the first step in receiving any gift from the Holy Spirit (including prophecy, miracles, healing, words of wisdom or knowledge, etc. [more in the next section]) comes from a *desire for the gift*.

1 Corinthians 12:31 tells us, "Now eagerly *desire* the greater gifts." While I mentioned earlier that some people do receive gifts automatically from God, not all do.

If everyone just "received it" on a whim, why would scripture tell us to *desire* the gifts? Why do we need to desire anything if we're set to receive it at some appointed future time anyway?

And if you're one of those people – like me – that didn't receive it on a whim, then you're going to have to *pursue* it.

I'll note here that not everyone will receive every gift, especially all at once. Even the verse right before the one I just shared says, "(30) Do all have gifts of healing? Do all speak in tongues? Do all interpret?"

Essentially the questions are rhetorical and the answer is 'no.'

After mentioning the 9 gifts of the Spirit, Paul says, "All these are the work of one and the same Spirit, and He distributes them to each one, just as He determines." (1 Corinthians 12:11 NIV)

Ultimately, it is up to God who gets what gifts — tongues included.

So does this mean don't ask for it?

I say no. You never know what gifts God will give you UNLESS you ask.

God is sovereign and the ultimate decision maker, but there's nothing in scripture saying we can't at least ask for the gift of tongues.

In fact, Paul encouraged it! He said the following about it:

- That it is a sign of the believer (Mark 16:17)
- It's the mark of a Holy Spirit filled Christian (Acts 2:4, & 19:6)
- It should not be forbidden (1 Corinthians 14:39)

I believe (and this is my opinion), that speaking in tongues is a great thing to desire, and in my experience, it has helped me grow in my relationship with Christ.

Is it required to be a strong Christian? No.

Will everyone get it? Probably not.

Do I feel closer to God in doing it? Yes.

And if you desire that, I want to help you if I can.

So first things first: **desire the gift**.

NEXT *SHOCKER* PRAY ABOUT IT

I know this is totally going to catch you off guard, but once you have the desire for the gift, now you need to pray that God will give it to you.

While we have established that God may not give it to you (even if for a while), it still doesn't hurt to pursue it.

Once I desired the gift, I had to ask the Holy Spirit for it. Over and over and over again. For months.

In fact, I've been saved 16 years or so, and I only recently received this gift. And even when I finally wanted the gift, I didn't get it right away. I had to keep asking.

I think one of the reasons God doesn't just give us what we ask for right away — even if its according to His will — is because he knows that once we have it, we're likely to stop praying because we got we wanted.

We say we won't but I know it's true…

Because I've done it.

Years ago, I started a business. It didn't take off right away. I prayed everyday for an outpouring of money. Eventually the business took off. I made hundreds and even thousands a day.

But as soon as the money started rolling in, I forgot about God. My prayer life and my Bible reading evaporated. I went from an hour a day of that to nothing at all. Months later, the business crashed, and didn't recover at all. I lost everything and I was out of work for quite some time.

It humbled me and who did I turn to when I was back at my lowest?

God.

I had to pray His forgiveness and mercy.

So we submit the request in prayer, expecting that He will hear us. Our prayers are NOT in vain. God hears every one of them.

Heck, he knows the request before we've made it! Psalm 139:4 says, "Before a word is on my tongue, you, LORD, know it completely."

And since the gifts of the Spirit are in accordance to God's will (as they bring people closer to God), he DEFINITELY hears us…

"This is the confidence we have in approaching God: that if we ask anything according to his will, he hears us." (1 John 5:14 NIV)

…And he acts accordingly:

"And if we know that he hears us—whatever we ask—we know that we have what we asked of him." (1 John 5:15 NIV)

But even still, praying one time for the gift of tongues is not enough. We may have to bring the request to God multiple times. I know I did.

If we truly desire something, we will pursue it until we have it. When I was courting my wife, I pursued her. I didn't just try once and give up. We called and texted and dated for months before getting engaged. The same is true when asking God for things to happen. We have to keep at it.

Jesus Himself gives us two parables that illustrate how we should approach prayer if we want to see God move in something.

The first is the persistent widow of Luke 18:1-5:

"Then Jesus told his disciples a parable to show them that they should always pray and not give up. He said: "In a certain town there was a judge who neither feared God nor cared what people thought. And there was a widow in that town who kept coming to him with the plea, 'Grant me justice against my adversary.'

"For some time he refused. But finally he said to himself, 'Even though I don't fear God or care what people think, yet because this widow keeps bothering me, I will see that she gets justice, so that she won't eventually come and attack me!'"

The second is the begging friend of Luke 11:5-10:

Then Jesus said to them, "Suppose you have a friend, and you go to him at midnight and say, 'Friend, lend me three loaves of bread; a friend of mine on a journey has come to me, and I have no food to offer him.' And suppose the one inside answers, 'Don't bother me. The door is already locked, and my children and I are in bed. I can't get up and give you anything.' I tell you, even though he will not get up and give you the bread because of friendship, yet because of your shameless audacity he will surely get up and give you as much as you need. "So I say to you: Ask and it will be given to you; seek and you will find; knock and the door will be opened to you. For everyone who asks receives; the one who seeks finds; and to the one who knocks, the door will be opened."

Jesus tells us that if we ask, it'll be given to us!

My point from these two illustrations is this: Keep asking the Holy Spirit to give you the gift if you really want it.

GETTING OUT OF YOUR OWN WAY

This is probably the most important part out of all this.

You see, years ago, I was alone in my townhouse, and I wanted the gift of tongues. I don't know why I wanted it, but I did.

There I was, praying, on my knees, asking God for that gift. The presence of the Holy Spirit was so heavy upon me that I was shaking and weeping.

I kept praying and praying.

Then I felt my tongue kind of move. It wriggled. Like it wanted to start speaking out.

So guess what I did?

I opened my mouth and...

Nothing came out.

I froze. I kept my tongue glued to the bottom of my mouth and I remained completely silent.

A minute or two passed by and the Spirit receded, and I collapsed; defeated and ashamed that I had stopped myself from encountering the Lord. I knew that I had been on the verge, and if I had tried, I might have gotten it.

But I let fear and doubt cloud my judgment and force me into silence.

I didn't try after that. Some small part of me still desired the gift, but I didn't really try because I figured it just wasn't for me. I tried to rationalize it away. And many of the people I knew at the time couldn't do it either, so why bother?

Years went by, and until earlier this year, I still hadn't really tried to do it.

But after a series of events that led to a deep desire and hunger for the Lord I have never known, the desire took root once more and I pursued it more passionately.

I started praying for it. I watched videos on how to do it (which were only somewhat helpful). I even fasted for a couple days.

I kept thinking what most people think: *that God will just give it to me at some point.*

And then, one day, I set out to try and do it.

I escaped the house and got in my car (where it was quiet and away from everyone). I prayed for the Holy Spirit to dwell in me, and give me the gift of tongues.

Then I just went for it.

I started off by just making the same couple of sounds over and over again. I felt something stir in me. I cleared my mind, prayed some more, and tried again.

This time, there were a few more "consonants" (or syllables) to it, but as I prayed and repeated the few that came to mind (or my lips, rather), I started to shake heavily like I did all those years before.

At first, I whispered the sounds repetitively. Then I recited them repeatedly at normal volume. My eyes welled with tears and my whole body shook with the Spirit.

In that moment, the presence of God came over me so strongly, I trembled. It was the strongest baptism of the Holy Spirit I have ever felt in my entire Christian walk. I repeated those sounds like a broken record, and while the Spirit was upon me, I went back in the house. I could hardly walk!

One after another, I put my hand on each of my kids' heads, and just prayed for a minute or so over each one in tongues. They were a little confused but they didn't question it.

I then stumbled into my bathroom where my wife happened to be standing. I didn't say a single English word — I just put my hands on her shoulders (somewhat for balance) and prayed over her for a couple minutes.

Then, just as quickly as it came, the Spirit receded and the tongues ceased.

I almost fell over when it left me I was so weak.

That was one of the greatest moments of not only my Christian walk, but of my entire life.

Now, I'd like to say that I spoke in tongues ever since…

But that's not true. Actually, it was another couple months before I could do it all the time, and here's why:

I doubted that it had all been real to begin with.

I don't understand why, we as humans, can see (or feel) God move in some way, and then later, doubt He was ever in the situation to begin with.

Why do we rationalize things away or remove God from our past experiences – assuming it WASN'T Him after all – even though we were beyond sure it WAS Him when it happened?

This is what I did.

Even though I had had that encounter with God, and it was amazing and unlike anything I had experienced up until that point and I can't tell you how awesome it was—

I still questioned whether it had been God or me speaking.

More specifically, I questioned whether the tongues had been "real" or if I had simply made it all up in my head.

You see, the enemy likes to put doubt in our head because if he can't get us to sin, then he'll settle for second best, and attempt to stifle our faith.

I allowed him to do that to me.

I fell for the lie that the tongues I had spoken weren't REALLY tongues, and I had simply imagined it.

How dumb does that sound?

But we do it all the time.

For months, I was conflicted. I was unsure if I should try again, or not. Had I been doing it wrong?

I was gripped – once again – by doubt and fear.

I was the person mentioned in James 1:7-8:

That person should not expect to receive anything from the Lord. Such a person is double-minded and unstable in all they do.

When I realized this, I knew I had one of two choices:

1. Give up on speaking in tongues altogether.
2. Go for it again, believing, with faith, that God would give it to me again, since he had already given it to me before.

I went for it.

This last time, I was determined. I watched a ton of videos about speaking in tongues and became thoroughly convinced that what I spoke would be the words of the Spirit, hands down.

I went into my approach with faith and boldness. I went in expecting for the Spirit to move.

And it did. However, I must share how it happened because I think this also ties into it.

So that afternoon, I went into my *secret place* to pray and finally receive it. (Matthew 6:6)

Initially, when I went in, I first asked God to search me of anything that was stopping me from receiving this gift from Him.

The word that came to mind was *forgiveness*. I prayed that He would forgive me of my sins, and I repented of any transgression (lingering sin).

I felt that the Spirit was nearby while I prayed, but His power wasn't "breaking through" you could say. Like I was on the verge of it taking over me, but something still blocked it. There stood an invisible barrier between us.

I then prayed deliverance on myself. Deliverance from pride and anger and greed. I won't go too far into it, as everyone's stance on it is different, but what I will say is this: I felt something lift off me. I believe I was freed of something.

The Spirit drew nearer still. Almost like a lingering presence I could feel in the room. It was as if the Holy Spirit was standing right next to me (and maybe He was). But there was still something blocking my breakthrough.

So I asked God, "God what is stopping me from feeling you fully?"

And He said to me: "You want to be forgiven, yet you yourself are holding onto unforgiveness."

That broke me. He was right (of course).

I had been holding onto a lot of unforgiveness, resentment, and bitterness towards a bunch of people. While I knew it was wrong, I just hadn't come to a place where I was willing to let those feelings go.

But in that moment, I realized that if it was the deciding factor on whether I could receive spiritual gifts from God or not, then I was willing to do so.

Now, I'm going to throw in one last, quick thing about this:

I was also dealing with a lot of money stress at the time. This has always been a struggle for me. I have been broke most of my life. I've never been poor or destitute (thank God), but I have been in debt my entire adult life. And I was not surrendering my debt stresses over to God — I was hanging onto them.

One thing I've learned recently is that God cannot take what we don't surrender. We can say we want God to move in certain things, but if we're still clinging to them, then he can't take the reins. It's like asking Him to drive, but still holding the steering wheel.

I had to make the choice to not only to forgive people of their trespasses, but also relinquish my financial struggles.

I said out loud, "I forgive everyone of everything. All debts paid in full."

That phrase – 'all debts paid in full' – was not something I came up with. It was a phrase that came to me, and I know now that it was of God, since the phrase was linked to both money AND forgiveness. It still gives me chills thinking about it.

And that was it.

Immediately after, the Spirit came upon me, and I started speaking in tongues for like 10-15 minutes straight.

And these 'sounds', while like the ones before, were somewhat different. I was overcome with gratitude and joy and love and peace.

I didn't care if I was doing it wrong or what it sounded like or what I was actually saying; I just kept speaking it as long as the Spirit allowed. I didn't let myself get in the way of my gift this time.

And now I can say that I have spoken in it ever since.

Over time, the syllables have changed, but the 'dialect' is the same. You just gotta try it, and not overthink it or get in your own head about doing it wrong.

If you're genuine, I think (again, my opinion) that God will honor it.

Praying in tongues has really deepened my relationship with the Lord. It's sort of elevated my prayer game.

But I want to throw out a disclaimer: Every gift is meant to bring glory back to God, not us.

While I love speaking in tongues now, and I'm grateful for it, I only want to continue doing it because I love God and want to praise Him in as many ways as I can. I don't want the gift for myself so I can appear "holier." All glory to God. Amen.

After having the gift, I wouldn't want to go back. I didn't know what I was missing until I had it. That's not to say you're not a "true believer" if you don't do it; it's just every person that I've talked to that CAN do it, has found it beneficial to their walk with Christ.

I'm sorry if I bored you with my lengthy story. My goal wasn't to do so.

However, I shared the whole thing in its entirety to highlight a few reasons why you may not be seeing the breakthrough of speaking in tongues if you've been desiring it:

- Fear of how you will sound
- Doubt that you'll be "doing it right"

- Belief that you don't deserve it
- The notion it's not for you and you'll never have it
- Possible unforgiveness, sin, or an area of your life you haven't fully surrendered to God yet and he wants you to make that sacrifice first

If I was to boil it all down into a step-by-step formula of how to approach trying to "activate" the gift of tongues, here's how I'd do it:

1. Desire the gift so bad you are willing to ask repeatedly for it.
2. Pray that God would give you the gift according to his will, and because he loves you.
3. Ask the Holy Spirit to "baptize you in Holy fire" (optional but it seems to work for some)
4. Request the Holy Spirit to search you and tell you if there are any areas of your life you need to surrender for a breakthrough.
5. Attempt to speak the "language of mysteries" without getting in your own way, allowing the devil to distract you, or overthinking it.

At that point, either the Holy Spirit will aid you in your attempt, you'll feel His presence, and you'll start speaking in an unknown language…

…Or…

…You won't feel anything at all.

At that point, you can either keep trying or come back to it.

God is more concerned with consistency than He is with intensity.

I've prayed over this book in hopes that you'll see that manifestation of the Spirit for God's glory and your walk!

HOW DO I KNOW THE TONGUES IS REAL?

I'll add this in as a final section. The rest you can find online through various resources.

I once heard Isaiah Saldivar —that Christian YouTuber I mentioned earlier—get asked this very question:

"How do I know if I'm actually speaking in tongues?"

And his answer was pretty accurate to my experience.
He said;

"You'll know it's real because you won't have to think of the sounds. They'll just come to you. And you can literally think of other things while you're speaking it."

This has been my case as well. When I pray in tongues, I don't need to think about 'what sounds I'll make.' I simply go right into it and start praying. I can literally think about nothing at all OR things of God while the sounds are pouring out of my mouth on autopilot.

And granted — this is a new language to me. I've only been doing it a couple months. So it's not like I'm "proficient" in it, or 'knew what to say or what sounds to make' when I started.

No. My mouth makes the sounds while my brain praises God or thinks about other things. A lot of the times, I'll basically have a conversation with God in my head while I speak in tongues outwardly. It's kinda cool.

The other point I want to make about tongues is the sounds you make.

Initially, the sounds you make will probably be like mine were at first: the same few syllables over and over again. And even now, there are times when the "words" I utter are repetitive.

I try not to correct it or "steer" the sounds in new directions. Have I done that? Yes. I'm human.

But what I've found is that the Holy Spirit tends to kind of override my attempts anyway. If I try to make certain sounds because I think it sounds too repetitive, He just takes back control and says whatever He wants.

Like I mentioned earlier, over time, the sounds will evolve or change randomly. That's good. If you're not doing it, then the Spirit is at work. Again, I try to be in control as little as possible.

Appendix B: Praying with Gifts

Well, I was going to end the book (again) after that last, last section, but I guess since I covered speaking tongues, I'll talk about my experience over the last couple months with some of the other gifts: words of knowledge, words of wisdom, healing, and prophecy (1 Corinthians 12:27-30).

In a previous chapter, I mentioned that I believe it is possible to have multiple gifts of the Spirit at differing times, and this happened to me. Specifically in one night:

About a month ago, I attended a young adult's event. I only went to help if they needed me, and it turned out, they didn't, leaving me with nothing to do.

What did I do with my time?

I prayed for people. I ended up praying for 3 people that night.

The first young man asked me to pray over his life and some of the things he was going through. One thing was his relationship with his dad.

When I prayed for him, a got a couple of words of wisdom that came up, and I mentioned them. He said that yes, he was dealing with those things. One of the things was his struggle to forgive his dad. I advised him that we are indeed commanded to forgive others of their sins (Colossians 3:13, Matthew 6:14-15), and he agreed he needed to.

As I was praying about this, I got a vision of his father coming to church (which his dad never has) because of his forgiveness.

Please know – I hardly ever get visions.

But I prophesied that over him.

The crazy thing about this is, he told me a few days later that when he got home that night, his dad (and mom) actually hung out and played a game together – which they hadn't done in years.

After him, I prayed for a middle-aged woman that I knew. Her mother had passed, and I asked if I could pray for her.

Now, in my head I already had an idea of the things I wanted to pray for her like comfort, and peace. But before I even started praying, I gave the Holy Spirit a few seconds to speak to me.

Within those few seconds, the word of wisdom "loneliness" came to mind.

I asked her if she was dealing with loneliness, and she almost started crying. In fact, her response was, "you hit the nail on the head with that."

Again, it was not something I had initially thought, but the Lord revealed it to me.

He also gave me words of knowledge to give her that I could pull from my experience or the Bible to help relate to her situation.

Lastly, I prayed for another lady that was dealing with some personal issues as well as kidney stones she'd had for months.

I first prayed for the personal issues. As I prayed for the things she asked, I received two words from God, "money" and, more oddly, "heaviness."

So I prayed against the attacks of the enemy via her finances. Then I prayed against a spirit of heaviness. She, too, started crying.

Afterwards, I prayed for complete healing for the kidney stones. A couple other ladies prayed for her as well after me.

Of course, there wasn't a good way to tell if the kidney stones were gone because the pain was still there.

But guess what – when she went to the hospital two days later for the surgery, the kidney stones were completely gone!

Praise Jesus!

Here's what I'll say about all this: God will move how He wants. That night was an exceptional night.

But over these past few months where I have truly made God the priority of my life, I have seen more instances of all the gifts (just at different times).

It all started happening after that night I was baptized in the Holy Spirit and received the gift of tongues!

I desired the gifts (and sought them), and God eventually gave them to me.

IDOLATRY OF GIFTS

I thank God for these past few days that I have been working on the update for this book, as I prayed for 7 people in 2 days, and I want to issue a word of caution (and I'll unpack it).

Here's the warning:

Avoid gift idolatry.

In other words:

We must desire *the gift giver* MORE THAN the gifts themselves.

It's great to desire the gifts of God. I still stand by what I wrote a couple pages back.

However, when you desire the gifts of God more than God Himself, two things happen:

1. Your prayers become all about you.
2. The gifts become the point of the prayer, and not the means to an end (bringing God glory).

Anything that we desire more than God, is considered an idol or a false God.

You've probably read the Ten Commandments, specifically Number One:

"You shall have no other gods before me. (Exodus 20:3)

Short version: Nothing comes before god. He's not just talking about other "gods," (demons, false deities) but idols as well (which is anything in creation) – including good things like His gifts.

I mentioned a little ways back about not expecting God to move in the way that WE want Him to, but just trusting that he will show up when we pray, regardless of the situation.

Well, the past few days I haven't really felt God's presence. It's been a proverbial dry spell.

And I've been itching to see those same manifestations of the Spirit like I did that night where all those gifts were present. But in my zealousness, I did the very thing I cautioned you not to do.

When I prayed for people, I expected major things to happen...

And when they didn't, I was discouraged.

Allow me to explain.

So there I was, already in a dry spell, (a couple weeks after that night of seeing all those gifts poured out) wanting God to do something. That night, Wednesday, I attended a youth event to help run one of the group tables.

The night went fine. Great message, genuine worship.

Afterwards, I ended up praying for 4 people: 2 youth, 2 adults.

And I have to be honest here:

As I prayed for them, I felt almost nothing.

Sure, I felt some compassion. But I didn't feel the Spirit move or speak to me in the midst of the prayers.

The people themselves came away crying almost every time, and thanked me for the prayers – which I should have taken as a sign that the Spirit had *moved in them* – but guess what?

I didn't care.

Nothing major happened. No deliverance or coming to Christ fully or words or images given to me by God for them.

Nothing.

Because God didn't speak or move the way I wanted, all of those prayers had felt like a waste of time to me. Like I had failed, even though the recipients were super grateful!

I'm not proud to admit that, but it gets worse.

The next day, after work, I was driving around, looking for this amputee veteran that hangs out at a local grocery store to pray for, since I felt like God had told me to pray for him.

He wasn't there, but a little ways down, I saw a homeless guy on a street corner, and I felt compelled to stop and give him some money.

Now, I don't say this for glory or praise, only to reiterate my stance on giving money to people as a means to pray for them.

I parked in a nearby lot, and spoke with him. Gave him the money. Then asked if I could pray for him. He agreed. He told me his story, and then I prayed for him.

I'll say this (and again, I'm ashamed to admit this, but I must): in my head, I told myself, "this guy's gonna get delivered of something." I already built up in my own head that I was going to cast a demon out of this guy.

I didn't even know if he HAD demons. But that's what I was determined to do.

In my prayer for him, I prayed against unclean spirits, strongholds, curses – all kinds of stuff like that.

No words or knowledge or prophecy or wisdom came to me. No revelations or visions. No deliverance.

And when nothing happened that I had hoped for, I walked away discouraged.

In that parking lot, there were a couple of other homeless guys. I asked them each if they wanted prayer.

First guy said no.

Second guy said yes. Same thing happened.

I prayed for massive things that I wanted God to do. Very little happened.

And granted – these grown men were also crying after my prayers for them.

So again – the Spirit was moving in them, not me.

(Proof that God can use anyone for his purposes, so don't ever think you aren't worthy or qualified to be used by God. I break that lie over you in Jesus' name right now. Amen.)

The last guy was a young man. He was not only homeless, but hooked on meth and fentanyl.

When I approached him for prayer, he said, "yes, but give me a second," and smoked some of his meth right there in the lot.

I waited for him to finish, then went into the prayer.

Side note: I'm not suggesting you go out and do this alone, but I wasn't concerned. I think of the following verses from Isaiah:

"No weapon forged against you will prevail, and you will refute every tongue that accuses you. This is the heritage of the servants of the Lord, and this is their vindication from me," declares the Lord. (Isaiah 54:17)

So do not fear, for I am with you; do not be dismayed, for I am your God. I will strengthen you and help you; I will uphold you with my righteous right hand. (Isaiah 41:10)

I didn't have any uneasy feelings about him. All I felt was his brokenness. And his honesty, honestly. (Lol.)

For this guy, I thought for sure I'd see something crazy happen. Demons. Instant healing of addiction. Being overcome by the Holy Spirit.

But nothing.

Actually, he stopped me mid-prayer, and said, "I appreciate you praying for me, but I shouldn't have had you do that while I'm high. Can you just come back and pray for me later?"

I was crushed. I didn't even get to complete my prayer.

I acquiesced and went home defeated.

I kept praying at home over the next day or so, asking God why I wasn't feeling anything. I asked Him what I was doing wrong.

Then, while I was praying, I realized what I had done. Random thought or God, I don't know but here's the revelation:

<u>I had prioritized seeing the gifts of God manifested *over* people knowing God loves them.</u>

I had put the gifts of God over God's presence…

And made them idols. I was worshipping the gifts, not the giver of the gifts.

I said out loud, "Lord. I have made your gifts my idol and I'm sorry."

Immediately I started weeping (and I'm not ashamed to admit it).

Finally I felt like I had broken through, and I was able hear from Him again. It took repenting and humility to get to that point.

What's crazy is He gave me a word right after that I think was meant for me to share with you that has to do with all this:

WHY YOU MAY NOT SEE THE GIFTS

God revealed to me that there were two interlinked reasons on why I don't see the gifts manifested at times:

1. I'm not ready.
OR
2. He's not ready.

Either, I'm not ready for the gifts (because my heart is in the wrong place) or He's not ready to allow me the gifts at this time (for whatever reasons He decides). Maybe a situation must resolve first. Maybe the recipient isn't ready to receive them. Maybe God wants me OR the listener to go through a season in our life that will bring us closer to Him first.

Who knows.

Point is: It's easy to get discouraged when we don't see the gifts of the Spirit manifest often (or ever).

Yet, even as I said before, God is sovereign and moves as He pleases. We have to respect and abide by that truth.

We can't just do whatever we want; we must "do what the father is doing," like Jesus did (John 5:19). And without the Spirit, we can, "bear no fruit without abiding in the vine." (John 15:4)

We must be Spirit led to do the will and works of the Father.

Here's what I'll say to wrap this up:

Desire the gifts, but don't put them on a pedestal (including tongues). They should be an outpoured result of our love of God. And if we take that same love for God, and show it to other people, the gifts will come eventually. I firmly believe that.

But we can't get angry or discouraged or overzealous and try to force things on people. We can't force prayer or deliverance on people, just as we can't force the Holy Spirit to pour Himself out upon us. We are God's servants – not the other way around.

I think at this point, that's all I got for you—
For real this time.

Once again, thank you for reading. I'm hoping and praying that you got something out of this.

If you're interested, I have another book called, "Illuminated by Grace" available. I'm in the process of writing a couple other books, so be sure to check in with me in the future.

God bless and good prayer.

Coty Schwabe

RECOMMENDED RESOURCES

There are a couple resources that have helped me grow in my ability to pray and relate to the Holy Spirit:

1. *Power Healing* **by John Wimber.** John Wimber, one of the founding leaders of the Vineyard movement, wrote this book and it really helped me understand that prayer isn't about us, but God using us to raise others up.

2. *Host the Holy Ghost* **by Vlad Savchuk.** I finished this book recently and it really convicted me on seeing the Holy Spirit not as just a "presence" of God, but an equal member of the Trinity, and how, by having a close relationship with Him, we are able to have the gifts of the Spirit as a result.

3. *Remnant Radio Podcast.* This is a podcast by three charismatic pastors – Josh Lewis, Michael Rowntree, & Michael Miller – who talk about spiritual gifts, and interview various religious leaders and voices on every end of the Christian spectrum. This podcast has really helped my wife and I see some different perspectives on the gifts of God, and it's really refreshing to break the echo chamber we can tend to lock ourselves into.

Complete Works by Coty Schwabe

CHRISTIAN NONFICTION

How to Pray Out Loud
Illuminated by Grace

POETRY BOOKS

bearing the burden of existence
flames, theft, and car crashes
the last light before extinction
life is an upward ascent
we're all just wanderers in the end
endless night of infinite dark

OTHER NONFICTION

A Student's Guide to Overcoming Procrastination
Call Center Survival Guide

NOTEBOOKS AND JOURNALS

Reverent Revelation Recorder (bible verse tracker)
Simple Men's Journal
hope returning, light restored (all white journal)
The Most EPIC Prayer Journal Ever (for kids)
Inspirational Bible Verse Journal
examining the you within (reflection journal)
Simple Sermon Notes Journal
hope fading, light obscured (all black journal)
Oversized Notebook (800 pages)
Poetry Journal

Printed in Great Britain
by Amazon